HAL•LEONARD
INSTRUMENTAL
PLAY-ALONG

AUDIO
ACCESS
INCLUDED

TRUMPET

JAMES BOND

T0070687

PLAYBACK+
Speed • Pitch • Balance • Loop

To access audio visit:
www.halleonard.com/mylibrary

Enter Code
3588-0681-9392-3685

Audio arrangements by Peter Deneff

ISBN 978-1-4950-6082-3

Music Sales America

EXCLUSIVELY DISTRIBUTED BY

7777 W. BLUEMOUND RD. P.O. BOX 13819 MILWAUKEE, WI 53213

Visit Hal Leonard Online at
www.halleonard.com

TITLE	PAGE
Diamonds Are Forever	4
For Your Eyes Only	5
From Russia with Love	6
Goldfinger	7
James Bond Theme	8
Live and Let Die	9
Nobody Does It Better	10
On Her Majesty's Secret Service	11
Skyfall	12
A View to a Kill	13
Writing's on the Wall	14
You Only Live Twice	15

DIAMONDS ARE FOREVER

from DIAMONDS ARE FOREVER

Words by DON BLACK
Music by JOHN BARRY

TRUMPET

FOR YOUR EYES ONLY

from FOR YOUR EYES ONLY

TRUMPET

Lyrics by MICHAEL LESSON
Music by BILL CONTI

FROM RUSSIA WITH LOVE

from FROM RUSSIA WITH LOVE

TRUMPET

Words and Music by
LIONEL BART

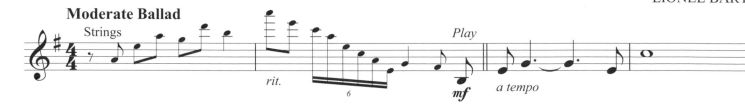

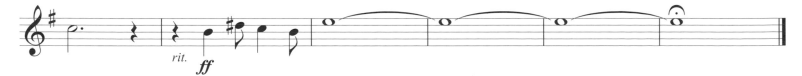

GOLDFINGER
from GOLDFINGER

TRUMPET

Music by JOHN BARRY
Lyrics by LESLIE BRICUSSE and ANTHONY NEWLEY

JAMES BOND THEME

TRUMPET

By MONTY NORMAN

LIVE AND LET DIE
from LIVE AND LET DIE

TRUMPET

Words and Music by PAUL McCARTNEY
and LINDA McCARTNEY

NOBODY DOES IT BETTER

from THE SPY WHO LOVED ME

TRUMPET

Music by MARVIN HAMLISCH
Lyrics by CAROLE BAYER SAGER

ON HER MAJESTY'S SECRET SERVICE - THEME

TRUMPET

By JOHN BARRY

SKYFALL
from the Motion Picture SKYFALL

TRUMPET

Words and Music by ADELE ADKINS
and PAUL EPWORTH

A VIEW TO A KILL

from A VIEW TO A KILL

TRUMPET

Words and Music by JOHN BARRY
and DURAN DURAN

WRITING'S ON THE WALL

from the film SPECTRE

TRUMPET

Words and Music by SAM SMITH
and JAMES NAPIER

YOU ONLY LIVE TWICE

from YOU ONLY LIVE TWICE

Music by JOHN BARRY
Lyrics by LESLIE BRICUSSE

TRUMPET